Charlotte FORTEN

Free Black Teacher

Charlotte
FORTEN
FREE BLACK TEACHER

by Esther M. Douty

GARRARD PUBLISHING COMPANY

Champaign, Illinois

Although many sources were consulted in the preparation of *Charlotte Forten: Free Black Teacher*, the biography is based primarily upon the original, handwritten, unpublished *Journal of Charlotte Forten*, on deposit at Howard University; upon my own two-year research on the Forten family of Philadelphia, part of which appeared in my biography of James Forten, *Forten the Sailmaker: Pioneer Champion of Negro Rights* (New York: Rand, McNally and Company, 1968); upon the valuable notes and introductory material in the published version of the *Journal of Charlotte Forten* by Ray Allen Billington (New York: Dryden Press, 1953); and upon *Personal Recollections of the Grimké Family* by Anna J. Cooper (privately printed, 1951).

Esther M. Douty

The editor and publisher acknowledge with thanks permission received to reprint on page 142 the last verse of "To Keep the Memory of Charlotte Forten Grimké" by Angelina Weld Grimké. Copyright by The Association for the Study of Negro Life and History.

Picture credits:

Culver Pictures: pp. 21, 32, 35, 75, 85, 90, 109, 126
Collection of Mrs. Esther M. Douty: pp. 9, 18, 96
Library of Congress: pp. 13, 56, 63, 98, 105, 112, 131
The Metropolitan Museum of Art, Rogers Fund, 1942: p. 26
Picture Collection, New York Public Library: pp. 29, 42, 49, 60
Schomburg Collection, New York Public Library: p. 117

Contents

1. Christmas Party 7

2. Byberry 16

3. A New Fear 25

4. A New School 36

5. The Promise 46

6. "A Parting Hymn" 58

7. Has My Dream Come True? 68

8. Dark Clouds 81

9. To the Sea Islands 97

10. The Tallest Tree in Paradise 111

11. "My Country! 'Tis of Thee" 123

12. Death of a Soldier 134

   Afterword 140

   Index 143

1. Christmas Party

"Charlotte! Robbie! Charley! Hattie! Henry!" Grandmother Forten's voice grew louder as she called each name. "For mercy's sake, stop that racing around and shrieking. And leave the Christmas presents alone. You know you're not allowed to open them until everybody is back from church. Your grandfather's not home yet. Neither are your fathers or your uncles."

Four-year-old Charlotte Forten, a thin child with a light brown skin and brown braids tied with a red ribbon, who *hadn't* been racing and shrieking, moved closer to the brightly wrapped gifts on the table. Her large brown eyes shone as she spied the storybook Grandfather Forten had promised her. She wished grandfather would hurry home. Perhaps if she looked out the window, she would see his tall, straight figure striding up the walk. But through the window she saw only a gray, wintery Philadelphia day and the big, three-story brick houses across Lombard Street.

The houses were much like the one she lived in with her grandparents, her parents, her brother Henry, three aunts, three uncles, and a changing number of runaway slaves who sought shelter with grandfather as they escaped toward freedom in Canada. Grandfather—James Forten, Sr.—had built and lived in the house since 1800, forty-one years earlier.

Disappointed at seeing only an empty street, Charlotte turned to watch the other children. Two-year-old Henry was banging his rag doll against grandmother's marble-topped sewing table. Her cousins Robert, Hattie, and "Baby Charley" Purvis were all trying to "play" the piano at once. From the kitchen came the

James Forten, Sr., Charlotte's grandfather, was one of Philadelphia's most respected citizens.

tempting fragrance of roasting goose and ginger spice.

All at once Charlotte felt very hungry. She ran to the kitchen to beg a cookie, but neither grandmother nor stately Aunt Sarah, busy creaming potatoes, had time for her.

Suddenly, happy shouts burst from the parlor. "Gracious, your grandfather and the others must be home," said grandmother, as she ladled plum sauce into a crystal bowl.

Charlotte raced to welcome the churchgoers. Uncle Robert Purvis pinched her cheek fondly. Grandfather's strong arms lifted her high. "Dear little Lottie," he said, pressing his brown face close to hers, "Christmas joy to you."

From her perch on grandfather's shoulder, she looked down admiringly at her father, Robert Bridges Forten, grandfather's second-born son. How handsome he was in his fawn-colored broadcloth suit. His face, the same light brown as Charlotte's, looked sad. It had looked sad for the past six months, ever since three-year-old Robert, Jr., had died of lung fever. But now her father managed to smile. "My, you're pretty as a Christmas candle in that red ribbon, Charlotte," he said, tugging her braids.

In the parlor the happy hubbub continued. "Christmas gifts!" Robbie Purvis' voice was the loudest. "Let's open the Christmas gifts!"

Grandmother came out of the kitchen. She said, "Run upstairs, Charlotte, and see if your mother feels well enough to come down."

Charlotte hurried up the wide staircase and

softly opened the door to the sitting room where her mother spent most of her time resting on a lounge. But today her mother was up, looking lovely in a rose silk gown whose full skirts hid her thinness. She had a coffee-with-cream complexion, and her brown eyes were very bright. She held out her arms. "Darling Lottie," she said, "just seeing you is a Christmas gift to me."

As they went down the stairs holding hands, Charlotte thought how much she loved her mother—more than anyone in the whole world, more even than grandfather.

The young Purvises were already unwrapping their presents when Charlotte and her mother entered the parlor. The children shouted with joy as marbles, dolls, tops, sugarplums, toy soldiers, balls, and books came into view. Charlotte dug happily into her pile of gifts. There was a big doll from mother and father, a book and a doll's tea set from her grandparents, and a blue silk pinafore from Aunt Margaretta.

From the dining room came the tinkle of a silver bell. "Ah ha," said Grandfather Forten.

"Grandmother is summoning us to dinner." He held out his arm to his oldest daughter, Margaretta, and in they all marched—twenty-three smiling people. Besides the Forten and Purvis families, there were two escaped slaves and three retired sailmakers from grandfather's sail loft.

They ate until they could eat no more of the roast goose and the roast suckling pig. They stuffed themselves with flaky rolls and creamed potatoes and onions and pickles and jellies and plum puddings and ice cream.

After dinner the table was cleared and set with little cakes, nuts, raisins, candies, and an enormous crystal bowl of punch. The Fortens were now ready for their friends, both black and white, to come Christmas calling.

In this year of 1841, as many white visitors as black crowded into the holly-decked, candle-lit home on Lombard Street. The Negro guests were good friends from Philadelphia's free Negro community, a sizeable group with great pride in its members. There were the Bustills, whose ancestor Cyrus Bustill, a baker for the Continental army, had been praised by George Washington. There were the Robert Douglasses, who for two generations had devoted their lives to setting up schools for black children. There were prominent Negro dentists, ministers, sailmakers from Grandfather Forten's sail loft, and dozens of bricklayers and carpenters, waiters, and owners of small businesses.

Among the white visitors were the sailmakers in James Forten's employ and the sea captains and great shipping merchants whose ships were

The Philadelphia waterfront, where Grandfather Forten's sail loft was located

outfitted with sails from his loft. Others were members of the Pennsylvania legislature, who admired Grandfather Forten for his lifelong struggle for laws that would assure fair treatment for the state's free Negroes. Many, such as James and Lucretia Mott, were abolitionists. They, like the Fortens and Purvises, were working to have slavery done away with, or abolished, in the United States.

But the white visitor who interested Charlotte most was a tall, gentle, dark-eyed man whom grandfather seemed to like very much. His name was John Greenleaf Whittier, and he was a Quaker and a poet. Many people called him "the poet of freedom" because so many of his poems concerned freedom for the slaves.

Charlotte trotted along with Mr. Whittier and held his hand as he spoke to the other guests. Suddenly she began to feel awfully sleepy. Before she knew it, grandfather was chuckling and carrying her upstairs to bed, saying, "Too much Christmas party for you, young lady. Maybe next year you can stay awake longer."

But there was no Christmas party at the Fortens the next year, for early in 1842 grandfather died.

The Philadelphia newspapers devoted considerable space to the death of the seventy-six-year-old sailmaker. They praised him as a patriot who had served in the American navy during the Revolution, and a man "whose strict honesty and pleasing manner made him many warm friends among our best citizens."

His funeral procession was one of the largest ever seen in Philadelphia. More than 3,000 persons, white and black, male and female, the richest and the poorest, walked slowly behind the funeral carriage to the graveyard of the African Episcopal Church of St. Thomas. This was the first Negro church in America. James Forten had helped to build it with his own hands in 1793.

Charlotte, trudging silently along with the others, felt a great sadness. But she was too young to realize fully that she would never see her grandfather again.

2. Byberry

James Forten had left the sail loft to his sons Robert and James, Jr., with the understanding that they were to take care of their mother and any of the women of the family who needed it. In the 1840s it was difficult for any woman to support herself, but especially a free Negro woman. About the only work open to her was that of house servant.

Though Sarah and Margaretta Forten were teachers, their pay was mostly the satisfaction they got from watching their black pupils grow up as educated persons. They received practically no money.

Neither Robert nor James was much interested

in the sailmaking business. Both were handsome, well-educated young men with a talent for singing, speaking, and writing. They lectured without pay before antislavery groups or wrote for the antislavery newspapers. Besides, the times were against them. In 1842 ships were beginning to use steam instead of sails for power. The sailmaking business everywhere declined. Soon the rich Forten family began to grow poor.

When Charlotte was almost five years old, her twenty-six-year-old mother died of tuberculosis, or as it was called then, lung fever. For days afterward Charlotte wouldn't eat, and cried so much that grandmother was alarmed.

"We've got to get Lottie away from here," she declared. "Let's send her to Byberry. I'm sure Harriet and Mr. Purvis will take her. That good country air and all those lively children will be the best thing for the child."

Robert Forten looked relieved. "I'll hitch up the horses and drive to Byberry right now," he said.

Uncle Robert Purvis (left) and his family welcomed Charlotte to their country home.

The next day Charlotte bounced happily on the seat beside father as they drove up the long, curving driveway to Uncle Purvis' beautiful country home. At the sound of the carriage wheels, Uncle Purvis, Aunt Harriet, and three of the Purvis children ran out of the wide doorway, waving and smiling.

"Welcome, Charlotte," said Aunt Harriet in her gentle voice, as she hugged the little girl close. Uncle Purvis pinched her cheek. Eight-year-old Robert, Jr., gave her a friendly grin. "Baby Charley" put his arms around her legs, and Hattie, who was about Charlotte's age, said, "Hi, Lottie. Come on up to the playroom. I'll show you my new dollhouse."

Charlotte ran off with Hattie, and father went to unload her valises. A short time later Charlotte bounded down the stairs to tell her father about Hattie's dollhouse, but father had already gone back to Philadelphia.

Her aunt saw her mouth crumple and said quickly, "Robert, why don't you and Hattie and Charlotte pick a pail of blackberries for supper? The south pasture is full of them."

Charlotte loved picking blackberries. In fact, she loved everything about Byberry. She loved going horseback riding with the Purvis children. She loved rambling through the woods and picking flowers in Aunt Harriet's gardens.

She especially enjoyed going with Uncle Purvis to look at the fine animals he raised on his estate. His Arabian horses, Durham cattle, and enormous hogs had won so many first prizes at county fairs that Byberry was known as one of the finest livestock farms in Pennsylvania.

All sorts of people visited Byberry. Some came to buy fine animals to stock their own farms. Others came and locked themselves away in Purvis' book-lined study. There they would plan how to fight the evil in America of men "owning" other men. She remembered seeing some of these antislavery people at her grandfather's, including bald-headed William Lloyd Garrison from Boston. His fiery abolitionist newspaper, *The Liberator*, had been kept alive by James Forten's money.

One day as Charlotte was playing on the front lawn, a familiar carriage rolled up the driveway. Charlotte looked up joyfully. "Father!" She rushed toward him. Then she saw the two women sitting stiffly in the back of the carriage. Their faces were hidden by sunbonnets.

"Quick, follow me," father said to the two. As they jumped out of the carriage, Charlotte saw torn trouser legs beneath the passengers' skirts. Why, they weren't women at all. They must be slaves escaped from their Southern masters.

20

Runaway slaves were part of the lives of all the Fortens and Purvises. Years ago Grandfather Forten and Robert Purvis had organized the Vigilant Committee of Philadelphia which guided and gave money to these fugitives as they made their perilous way toward Canada and freedom.

Later the Vigilant Committee became the Underground Railroad, with secret "way stations" for escaped slaves throughout the nation. Almost every week some frightened, hungry,

Runaway slaves like these were a part of young Charlotte's everyday life at Byberry.

ragged runaway was fed, clothed, and sheltered in the hidden room beneath the kitchen at Byberry or in the secret attic in the Forten's Philadelphia home.

When father returned from having the fugitives taken care of, he said, "Charlotte, your grandmother wants you home for your birthday. She's planning something nice for you."

But before Charlotte's fifth birthday on August 17, a dreadful incident took place—one that she never forgot. She and father went to a parade to celebrate the freeing of the slaves in the West Indies. Most of Philadelphia's Negroes were there, watching or marching proudly behind bright flags and a lively band of music. Suddenly a mob of hoodlums rushed out of a side street and beat the marchers with clubs and stones. The marchers fought back. Soon many people, white and black, lay groaning on the cobblestones.

Then came the terrible cry: "Burn them out." With a yell, the mob turned and ran toward the Negro section of the city.

"Charlotte! Home quick!" Father scooped her into his arms and raced toward their house. From the next street came sounds of the mob breaking into Negro homes. A church went up in flames. Stores were plundered.

At 92 Lombard Street Grandmother Forten met her son and granddaughter at the door. "You don't have to tell me," she said angrily. "Another riot. I can hear the mob yelling from here."

Father nodded grimly, dashed to the hall cupboard, and brought out a shotgun. Then he sat down on the stairway facing the front door, ready to shoot the first intruder. Outside, the cries of the rabble grew wilder as it surged toward the Forten home.

Charlotte felt cold with fear. She hid herself in grandmother's skirts, but grandmother, peering through the shutters, appeared not to notice her.

Then suddenly other sounds drowned out the noise of the mob. Cannon fire. Horses' hooves clattering on the cobblestones. Robert Forten stood up. He wiped the sweat from his forehead.

"The militia. Thank God, they've called out the militia to put down the mob. We'll be safe for a while anyway."

"Safe?" Charlotte did not understand. "But why do those men want to hurt us, father?"

Grandmother answered. "Poor, ignorant creatures," she said bitterly. "They hate us because our skin is dark."

This was the first time that Charlotte thought about the color of her skin. Or about the color of anybody's skin.

3. A New Fear

By the time that Charlotte was eleven years old, life in the big house on Lombard Street had changed. Only grandmother, Aunt Margaretta, teen-aged uncles Thomas and William, and Charlotte herself lived there now. Her brother Henry was living with another aunt, and the rest of the family had moved away. Her father, however, was not far off, for he had sold the sail loft and bought a farm in nearby Bucks County. Here a neighbor wrote of him:

"Robert B. Forten is an amateur farmer, a gentleman of fine education, a pure chaste poet, and attends to farming for love of nature."

A group of black workmen in Philadelphia, as
drawn by a Russian visitor in the early 1800s

Sometimes Charlotte and Henry visited their father in the country, but it wasn't much fun. Father was kind but he paid them little attention. When he wasn't riding horseback over his land, he was writing poetry, or playing the piano, or just sitting and thinking. Both children were glad to get back to Philadelphia.

One thing Robert Forten made clear: *Charlotte must be educated at home*, even though there were several schools for black children in Philadelphia. In fact, Margaretta Forten taught at Sarah Mapps Douglass' school, the finest of the group. But father was against segregated education and refused to send his daughter to an all-Negro school.

He also believed that conditions in Philadelphia were growing more dangerous for black people. Lombard Street had changed for the worse. In James Forten's day it was mainly a street of good homes in which well-to-do Negroes lived. Now it was becoming a slum, crowded with poor blacks.

Most of these people were free, but some were

runaway slaves. Unable to find jobs, some of the newcomers turned to crime. Black people as well as white were afraid of these criminals. Unfortunately, many white people began to fear any Negro they did not personally know. This made it hard for the majority of black people, who were hardworking and law-abiding.

To make matters worse, another violent race riot had recently taken place, sparked by ill-feeling between Irish immigrants and Negroes, who were seeking the same jobs. Again Negro houses were burned, and black and white men killed and injured. The militia had to be called out twice before the city quieted.

Robert Forten made his mother promise to keep Charlotte home where she would be safe. He would take her to live with him, he said, when his nerves were in better shape.

Charlotte didn't mind going to school at home since Aunt Margaretta was a fine teacher, but she was lonesome. She spent a great deal of time, perhaps too much time, reading. "Leave the books alone, child," grandmother would urge.

"Go out in the garden and roll your hoop."

But Charlotte found it hard to leave the books in Grandfather Forten's library alone. She read history books, travel books, books and newspapers about abolition, and poetry, which she liked best of all.

Her favorite was a collection of unpublished poems written by members and friends of her family. She loved the poem that John Greenleaf Whittier had written for her aunts, Margaretta, Sarah, and Harriet, in 1833. The young poet and William Lloyd Garrison had come to

Whittier was a well-known foe of slavery and a loyal friend of the Forten family.

Philadelphia in that year to meet with Robert Purvis, Lucretia Mott, and others to form the American Anti-Slavery Society.

Later, Whittier thought about the Forten women. They were charming, refined, well-educated, with beautiful manners. They could trace their family in Pennsylvania back for four generations. Their father was wealthy and respected. Yet because they were black, they were treated with scorn by many who were beneath them in character, education, and refinement. One night Whittier couldn't sleep until he had set down his thoughts in a poem called, "To The Daughters of James Forten."

And what, my sisters, though upon your brows
The deeper coloring of your kindred glows
Shall I less love the workmanship of Him
Before whose wisdom all our own is dim?
Shall my heart learn to graduate its thrill?
Beat for the White, and for the Black be still? . . .
Still are ye all my sisters, meet to share
A Brother's blessing and a Brother's prayer.

Another of Charlotte's favorites was the poem

that Aunt Sarah had written in 1833 for a convention of antislavery women in New York.

We are thy sisters, God has truly said,
That of one blood the nations he has made.
O Christian woman! in a Christian land,
Canst thou unblushing read this great command?
Suffer the wrongs which wring our inmost heart,
To draw one throb of pity on thy part!
Our skins may differ, but from thee we claim
A sister's privilege and a sister's name.

Every once in a while Charlotte would write some verses herself, but she kept this a secret. She did not think they were good enough to show to anyone.

When she was twelve years old, Charlotte accompanied Aunt Margaretta to the meetings of the Philadelphia Female Anti-Slavery Society. Here she became friendly with Sarah and Angelina Grimké. These great-spirited women had fled from their family's rich cotton plantation in South Carolina because they could not accept the horrors of slavery. Now they gave time to helping the slaves win freedom.

Charlotte learned about Frederick Douglass (at left) and other workers in the antislavery movement.

At the meetings Charlotte would sit quietly, her large eyes over-solemn for a child's. Antislavery talk swirled about her, and she listened to it with her mind and heart. The antislavery women were always trying to raise money to aid runaway slaves and to help *The North Star*, the abolitionist newspaper published by a brilliant, brave, former slave named Frederick Douglass.

In 1850 the customary way for these women to raise money was to hold a fair. For months before the event, they made aprons, nightgowns, and baby dresses. They embroidered, knitted, crocheted, and tatted useful and useless articles. They begged for needlework from antislavery sympathizers in Europe. They painted pictures on velvet and made cakes, candy, and jelly. The money from the sales was used for the benefit of the slaves.

At the fairs, Charlotte and Hattie Purvis would run from booth to booth, admiring the pretty articles and sampling the good things to eat. Charlotte glowed when someone bought a red velvet pincushion that she herself had made. When she was happy like this, with shining eyes and face alight with a smile, people said that Charlotte Forten was really quite pretty, especially since her slender figure was graceful, and she held herself straight and proud.

Soon after Charlotte's thirteenth birthday, a special fear gripped Philadelphia's Negroes. In that year, 1850, Congress passed the Fugitive

Slave Act which stated that an escaped slave must be returned to his owner. Frequently a generous reward was offered for the return of a slave so that slave-catching became a profitable business. Now unscrupulous men watched not only for escaped slaves but for any free Negro who could not prove that he was free. Often black children were kidnapped, taken to a Southern port, and sold as slaves.

Charlotte's father, living a quiet life on his Bucks County farm, grew uneasy about his daughter. One day in 1853 he came to see grandmother and Aunt Margaretta.

"Charlotte must leave Philadelphia," he declared. "Now that she's old enough to work, I'm afraid someone will steal her and sell her South."

"But where will she go?" worried grandmother. "You say you don't feel able to raise a girl by yourself."

Then Margaretta spoke quietly. "I've been thinking for some time," she said, "that Charlotte has learned all I can teach her. With

Robert Forten knew that under the new Fugitive
Slave Act even free blacks were often snatched
from their homes and sold as slaves.

her fine mind, she should have the best education she can get. Let's send her to Massachusetts,
to Salem. The excellent Higginson School there
accepts girls of our race. She can live with the
Remonds."

"The Remonds of Salem!" Father clapped his
hands enthusiastically. "Why didn't I think of
that?"

4. A New School

Salem! Sixteen-year-old Charlotte knew that the old Massachusetts town was beautiful and thriving, with elegant, square-shaped houses set on broad, tree-lined streets. Swift clipper ships, Salem-built and Salem-manned, sailed the seven seas and brought back fortunes in spices and sugar, coffee and silks to its great merchant-shippers.

In 1854 Salem's people were mostly anti-slavery. The public schools admitted children of every color, and black residents as well as white drilled as militiamen on the town common. Years earlier, numbers of well-educated free

Negroes had settled there, opened small businesses, and prospered.

The best known of this group were Charles Remond and his sister Sarah, who were lecturing agents for the Massachusetts Anti-Slavery Society. Charles Remond, a powerful speaker, had in 1840 been sent to London as a delegate to the World Anti-Slavery Convention. He stayed in England for two years, speaking to huge audiences on the tragedy of America—slavery. When he returned home, many Americans, black and white, regarded him as the nation's most prominent Negro.

Sarah Remond was not a fiery speaker like her brother, but her voice was sweet, clear, and quiet. She was unusually well educated for a woman of her time, of whatever color, and she spoke with such sincerity and common sense that her lectures won thousands of people to the cause of abolition.

It was just noon when the train carrying Charlotte and her father puffed into the railroad station at Salem. Charles Remond, his wife, and his sister Sarah were waiting on the platform.

Charlotte stared respectfully at the famous Charles. She saw a well-dressed man, about forty-four, with a medium-brown complexion. He was small and thin but athletic-looking. His movements were quick, and she could tell that he expected people to pay a lot of attention to what he said. Sarah, somewhat younger, was taller, with a lively, friendly face. The sight of Mrs. Remond made Charlotte's heart jump. She reminded her of her "own dear lost mother."

Charlotte liked the Remond home on Dean Street. It was not as fine and spacious as the Forten home in Philadelphia, but it was well furnished and large enough for Charlotte to have her own room, which overlooked an old-fashioned flower garden.

Beyond the garden Charlotte could see other quiet, tree-shaded streets. Which one of these, she wondered, led to the Higginson School for Girls? And which led to the Remond Hair Works where the family earned its living by weaving wigs and hair pieces for men and women?

In the morning her father walked with her to school. As they picked their way over the uneven old brick sidewalks, he said, "You know, Charlotte, there are 188 girls at the school. You will be the only one who isn't white."

"Yes, father, I know." Charlotte's gentle voice was a bit sharp. Father had told her this before. So had her aunts. And her grandmother. And the Purvises. And the Anti-Slavery Society ladies. She was tired of hearing it. Then a glance at her father's face made her say, as she always did, "Don't worry. I'll study hard. I'll prove to the others that a dark skin does not mean a second-rate mind."

At the school, the principal, Miss Mary Shepard, greeted them cordially. Her gray blue eyes were wise and kind. Charlotte liked her.

Miss Shepard seemed surprised that Charlotte was so advanced in her studies. "Your aunt has taught you well," she said. "If you study hard, I believe you can graduate in a year."

On the way home from school Charlotte bought a composition book with a black and white cover. On the cover she printed in large letters "JOURNAL."

Her first entry, dated May 24, 1854, read:

Rose at five. The sun was shining brightly through my window, and I felt vexed with myself that he should have risen before me. . . . How bright and beautiful are these May mornings! The air is so pure and balmy, the trees are in full blossom, and the little birds sing sweetly.

I stand by the window listening to their music, but suddenly remember that I have an arithmetic lesson which employs me until breakfast; then to school. . . . After dinner practised a music lesson, did some sewing, and then took a pleasant walk by the water. . . . On my way home, I stopped at Mrs. Putnam's, and commenced reading *Hard Times*, a new story by Dickens. Father left yesterday for Providence and New Bedford. Thinks he will return tomorrow evening.

But Robert Forten did not return to Salem

the next evening. He went instead to Boston where the arrest of Anthony Burns, a fugitive slave from Virginia, had thrown the city into turmoil.

It was not the first time that Boston had been stirred up over a runaway slave, for as Charlotte had been disappointed to learn, slavery had many friends there. The important textile industry in Massachusetts depended upon cotton from the South, which was raised with slave labor. Southern planters and their families were favorites with Boston society. And in 1850 when Congress passed the Fugitive Slave Act, 100 guns had boomed a joyous salute across the Boston Common.

Still, most Bostonians hated slavery. They considered it disgraceful that the federal government had passed a law which ordered all citizens to aid the federal marshals in arresting a runaway slave and which heavily fined anyone helping a slave to escape.

Anthony Burns denied that he was an escaped slave. Many Bostonians believed him and were angry at his arrest. They milled through the streets, shouting for his release. To keep him "safe" until his trial, the government locked Burns in the federal courthouse and ordered the streets patrolled by armed troops.

These measures did not prevent T. W. Higginson, a Unitarian minister, and a number of prominent citizens from storming the courthouse in an effort to rescue Burns. They failed. In the confusion a federal marshal was killed.

Flanked by marshals, Burns watches from a window as federal troops hold back an angry mob.

After that, both federal and state troops guarded the prisoner, whose trial was to begin the following Monday.

In nearby Salem, Charlotte Forten tried to keep her mind off Anthony Burns. She spent Saturday morning sweeping, dusting, and sewing. She spent the afternoon with her teacher looking at engravings of European scenes, a pastime which was popular with fashionable young ladies in 1854.

But it was no use. "I can scarcely think of anything else," she wrote in her journal. On Wednesday Charlotte, Sarah Remond, and Mrs. Caroline Putnam, a friend of the family, went to Boston to join the crowds still thronging the streets and shouting for Burns' release.

She knew that her father was somewhere in the city helping to raise money for Burns' defense, but she didn't see him until that night when she was invited to dinner at the home of the fiery editor of *The Liberator*.

"Dined at Mr. Garrison's," she scribbled happily before going to bed. "At the table I watched earnestly the expression of that noble face. . . ." She was so happy that she almost forgot about Burns.

But then the federal court ruled that Burns was an escaped slave and must be sent back to his master in Virginia. He was marched down State Street to a waiting ship through groaning, hissing lines of people. Thousands of federal troops, state militia, and the entire police force guarded him to prevent any attempt at rescue.

Charlotte took the news badly. "Poor Burns," she wrote, "has been sent back to a bondage worse, a thousand times than death. . ." She thought the government was cowardly to send thousands of soldiers to satisfy the demands of the slaveholders and to "deprive of his freedom a man, created in God's own image, whose sole offense is the color of his skin." She ended her entry, "A cloud seems hanging over me, over all our persecuted race, which nothing can dispel."

By Sunday Charlotte felt better. She noticed the weather. "A beautiful day. A delicious breeze fans my cheek as I sit by the window writing."

Her eye fell on her school books. She thought a moment, and then began again to write slowly. "Although [I am] much saddened by recent events, yet they shall be a fresh incentive to more earnest study, to aid me in fitting myself for laboring in a holy cause, for enabling me to do much towards changing the condition of my oppressed and suffering people."

Charlotte's face looked determined as she closed her journal. Now she knew what she was going to do with her life.

5. The Promise

Early the next morning Charlotte's father came to say good-bye.

"You'll be back soon, won't you, father?" Charlotte asked hopefully. Her heart was set on their living together in a little New England home with a bright garden and a white picket fence around it.

"I don't know what I'm going to do, Charlotte," Robert Forten answered. "When I know, I'll write you."

At first Charlotte watched the mails for some word from her father but none came. She tried not to think about it. She was busy from dawn until the candle burned low in her bedroom each night. A day's activities went like this:

She rose very early, studied her lessons, and then went to school. There, in addition to her classwork, she and her best friend, Lizzie Church from Nova Scotia, graded papers for Miss Shepard. After school she talked with her teacher about slavery and prejudice. "I fully appreciate her kindness and sympathy with me," she told her journal. "She wishes me to cultivate a Christian [forgiving] spirit in thinking of my enemies; I know it is right, and will try to do so, but it does seem so very difficult."

Returning home, she read *The Liberator*, ironed, and practiced her piano lesson. Later she baked bread and read a sermon by the abolitionist minister Theodore Parker.

It was no wonder that Charlotte began to suffer from headaches. Her remedy was to take the Remond dog Dash for a walk. She loved to walk along the nearby beach admiring "the beautiful fleecy, floating clouds, islands of pearl on a sea of blue."

Sometimes she would walk at night and think of her family in Pennsylvania. "The moonlight, the perfect stillness, broken only by the chirping of crickets reminded me of my country home," she wrote once, "and my thoughts turn to the loved ones there with whom I have enjoyed so many quiet, lovely evenings like this. I imagine myself again sitting with father and mother on our pleasant porch, listening to the merry voices of my dear little brothers."

Like most young girls, Charlotte was given to moods. Often she was joyous, sometimes sad. It didn't take much to set her off into one or the other. One morning she watched a robin from her window and wrote: "a robin redbreast perched on the large apple tree in the garden, warbles his morning salutation in my ear;— music far sweeter to me than the clearer tones of the Canary birds in their cages, for they are captives, while he is free! *I* would not keep even a bird in bondage."

Not even a bird in bondage. Charlotte's mind was seldom far from the plight of her people.

Salem in 1854 was a quiet New England town of pleasant houses and tree-shaded streets.

The following day brought her more unhappiness. "I have suffered much today," she confided to her journal. "My friends Mrs. Putnam and her daughters were refused admission to the Museum, after having tickets given to them, solely on account of their complexion. Insulting language was used to them—of course they felt and exhibited deep, bitter indignation, but of what avail was it? None, but to excite the ridicule of those contemptible creatures, miserable doughfaces who do not deserve the name of men. No words can express my feelings. But these cruel wrongs cannot be much longer endured."

She was still downcast at school the next morning. Perhaps Miss Shepard noticed her sadness, for she brought out an album that always delighted Charlotte—pictures of England. As usual, Charlotte was enchanted.

That night she wrote, "Oh, England! My heart yearns toward thee as to a loved and loving friend. I long to behold thee, to dwell in one of thy quiet homes, far from the scenes of my early childhood; far from the land, my native land—where I am hated and oppressed because God has given me a *dark skin*."

When Charlotte got home from school the next day, Mrs. Remond handed her a letter. Charlotte's heart jumped at the sight of the handwriting. At last her father had written.

The letter was short. Father did not want to live in New England, not even in a little white house with Charlotte. Prejudice against Negroes, he wrote, was as strong there as in Philadelphia. In fact, her father said, he was thinking of moving to Canada, and then later perhaps to England—permanently.

England! Charlotte whirled happily on her toes. If father moved to England, surely she would go with him.

Several months later, on a sunless October afternoon in 1854, the crunch of carriage wheels on the Remond driveway brought Charlotte excitedly to the front door. It was the Remonds, bringing with them an important house guest. Charlotte's glance went to the strong-featured, dark-skinned man getting out of the carriage. She was disappointed. He looked so—so ordinary.

Yet she knew that William Wells Brown was a great man. He had been a slave for twenty years in Kentucky and Missouri. Then he had escaped and found work on the steamboats plying the Great Lakes. As a seaman, he had managed to smuggle many slaves to Canada and freedom. During these years he had trained himself as a speaker. The New York Anti-Slavery Society sent him to England and the Continent as a lecturer for abolition.

In Europe he gave over a thousand lectures to enthusiastic crowds. He wrote several widely read books. Famous people sought his company. But William Wells Brown could not return to his native land, for he was still a slave. Under the Fugitive Slave Act he would be arrested and sent back to his master. Then in 1854 his friends bought his freedom. Brown hurried home to continue his battle against slavery. He left his daughters in Europe, the older to teach in England, the younger to study in France.

Perhaps Charlotte reminded Brown of his daughters, for as the days passed, he talked to her constantly—about his family, about how she must never stop working to gain freedom for the slaves, and about England. England! Perhaps this time next year, Charlotte thought happily, she would be living in that country with her father, far from the prejudice that made her so unhappy.

Meanwhile Brown joined others in telling her she *had* to do well right here in Higginson School. Every lesson she learned was a triumph not only for herself but for the oppressed Negro people. By excelling in her studies she could help prove to an unfriendly world that blacks were as capable as whites. *She must excel.*

This was a lot of responsibility for a girl who had just turned seventeen, a girl who, like other girls her age, enjoyed a good time. Often she was just plain sick of studying. Then if it was fruit season, she would put on her bloomer costume, climb a cherry tree in the Remond's orchard, and pick enough cherries to make the family a juicy pie. Or she would go horseback riding with Mr. Remond, who was a skilled horseman.

In winter the Remonds changed their carriage for a sleigh. Charlotte loved the sleigh rides by moonlight when the snow glistened like millions of diamonds and the stars twinkled huge and brilliant overhead. She enjoyed the snowball fights and the coasting with her schoolmates which sent her glowing and laughing to warm up by the great fireplace in the schoolroom.

Some evenings she would join the cheerful little party around the fire in Mrs. Remond's room and listen while Mrs. Remond read poetry. Then they sang or played whist or talked of the trips they would take in America when the slaves were free.

Charlotte's favorite pleasure in any weather was walking along the beach at Marblehead with Miss Shepard and Lizzie Church. Once Nathaniel Hawthorne's sister walked with them and gave her an unusual stone to remember the place by.

Later, as Charlotte recalled these walks, she wrote: "It was here that I first saw the sea, and stood entranced in silent awe, gazing upon the waves as they marched in one mass of the richest green to the shore, then suddenly broke into foam, white and beautiful as the winter snow."

Her friends the Putnams gave many parties. Boys and girls were often invited for an evening of music, conversation, games, and dancing. Charlotte loved to dance and went to some of the parties. "I was ashamed," she said afterward, "to steal so much time from my studies."

On Christmas Day 1854, Charlotte was homesick. She wrote in her journal, "I imagine that I can see Grandmother's loved countenance as she listens to the happy voices of the little ones around her wishing her a 'Merry Christmas.' I think of them all, and cannot help wishing that I could make one of the happy group assembled there. . . ."

To raise her spirits she read an old letter from Aunt Margaretta. The letter was kind and cheering, like hearing Aunt Margaretta's gentle voice. The letter also reminded Charlotte of her promise to send her aunt a list of the books she had read during the past year.

On New Year's Day 1855 Charlotte listed almost a hundred books. There were three volumes of *The Queens of England*, several volumes of Macaulay's *History of England*, a history of Scotland, the works of Scott and

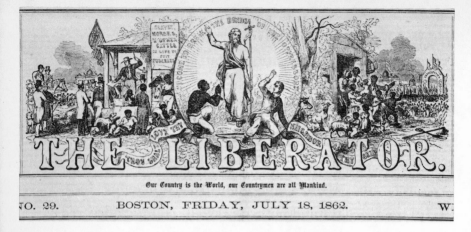

NO. 29. BOSTON, FRIDAY, JULY 18, 1862. W.

The masthead of *The Liberator*, William Lloyd Garrison's fiery abolitionist newspaper

Dickens, and many other books that were considered the best literature of the day. Since Charlotte was being educated as many fashionable young American ladies were in those days, the books she read dealt mostly with British history and were by British authors. She learned little American history and read few American authors except the poems of her beloved Whittier and the novel *Uncle Tom's Cabin* by Harriet Beecher Stowe.

Charlotte also read books and newspapers that her schoolmates and her teachers had probably never heard of. She read every issue

56

of *The Liberator* and the other antislavery papers. She read the poems of a Massachusetts slave, Phillis Wheatley, who had lived in George Washington's time, and she read the writings of the antislavery writers Lydia Maria Child and Isaac Hopper who had collected information about outstanding black men and women and their achievements.

When she learned about these heroic Negroes, Charlotte felt proud. She promised herself that, when she was a teacher, she would make sure that every black child learned about Phillis Wheatley, Jean Baptiste Point du Sable, Peter Salem, Paul Cuffe, Richard Allen, Absalom Jones, James Forten, and the many other black people who had given much to America.

As she wrote her New Year letter to her aunt, Charlotte realized that she had only a few more weeks at the Higginson School, for in February her class was to be graduated.

6. "A Parting Hymn"

Graduation Day was bitter cold, with blowing snow. The school auditorium was crowded. People were standing in the back of the room. Charlotte Forten, pretty in her white dress, sat on the stage with the other members of the graduating class. She was happy. She had passed all examinations with honors. Even the public questioning had gone well.

Charlotte had dreaded this public examination when, according to custom, anyone could attend and ask a pupil any question he liked. Usually the questions were easy, but sometimes a mean person would ask a tricky question so that the pupil would become embarrassed and perhaps cry. However, in February 1855 no mean person appeared. All the girls did well. Miss Shepard's eyes shone with pride.

Now all that remained of the graduation exercises was the announcement of the author of the prize-winning commencement hymn. The poem, called "A Parting Hymn," had already been printed and given to the audience, but no one except its author knew who had written it.

Here is how William Wells Brown described the scene: "After the singing of the hymn the principal said, 'Ladies and gentlemen, the beautiful hymn just sung is the composition of one of the students of this school, but who the talented person is, I am unaware. Will the author step forward?'

"A moment's silence, and every eye was turned in the direction of the principal, who seeing no one stir, looked around with a degree of amazement. Again she repeated, 'Will the author of the hymn step forward?' A movement among the female pupils showed that the last call had been successful. The buzzing and whispering throughout the large hall indicated the intense interest felt by all. 'Sit down. Keep your seats,' exclaimed the principal, as the crowd rose to its feet or bent forward to catch a glimpse of the young lady, who had now reached the front of the platform.

"Thunders of applause greeted the announcement that the distinguished authoress before them was Charlotte L. Forten. Her finely-chiseled features, well-developed forehead, countenance

William Wells Brown, a noted abolitionist, was at Charlotte's graduation.

beaming with intelligence, and her dark complexion, showing her identity with an oppressed and injured race, all conspired to make the scene an exciting one."

Happy tears came to Charlotte's eyes as the audience stood and again sang "A Parting Hymn."

> *When Winter's royal robes of white*
> *From hill and vale are gone,*
> *And the glad voices of the spring*
> *Upon the air are borne,*
> *Friends who have met with us before,*
> *Within these walls shall meet no more. . . .*
>
> *May those, whose holy task it is,*
> *To guide impulsive youth,*
> *Fail not to cherish in their souls*
> *A reverence for truth;*
> *For teachings which the lips impart*
> *Must have their source within the heart. . . .*

Three weeks after graduation a cold rain seeped through Charlotte's mackintosh as she again returned empty-handed from the post office. Oh, *why* wouldn't father answer her letter? He knew that she planned to be a teacher. In fact, that was what he had always wanted her to be. But he had not answered her request for permission to enter the Salem Normal School so that she could become a *trained* teacher. He must know that the money grandmother had sent her was almost gone, and that grandmother could send no more. How, Charlotte worried, did he expect her to pay the Remonds for her room and board if he sent her no money?

The Remonds were teaching her to weave hair for wigs, and occasionally she kept store for the Putnams, but what she earned barely allowed her to replace her worn-out clothing.

She had already passed the examinations for the Normal School. Mr. Richard Edwards, the principal, was kind and encouraging and had entered her name on the school register.

"I want you to attend classes, Miss Forten," he told her. "Otherwise you will fall behind the other scholars in your work. I'm sure you will hear favorably from your father in a few days."

But the "few days" went by, and there was

This placard advertised the Remond Hair Works.

no word from father. Then on a windy March day the letter came. "It costs too much money for you to stay in Salem," her father had written. "Come home as soon as possible."

Charlotte was too upset to think. She felt that the only person who would really understand was Miss Shepard. She hurried to her teacher's tiny cottage to show her father's note. Miss Shepard was distressed.

"You *must* not leave, Charlotte. You owe it to yourself and to your people to become a trained teacher. *Please* let me lend you the money. You can pay me back when you have a teacher's salary."

How kind Miss Shepard is, Charlotte thought, but I cannot accept her offer—she has so little herself. Besides how can I be sure that I—a black woman—will be hired as a teacher anywhere?

As if in answer to her question, Mr. Edwards came to see her. "I hope you can stay with us, Miss Forten," he told her again. "Please write your father that I can *promise* you a teaching position here in Salem if you graduate from the Normal School."

Charlotte nodded her thanks. She was afraid she would cry if she tried to say anything. Ten days later, to her joy, her father sent part of the money she needed for expenses. "I thank Father very much for his kindness," she wrote, "and am determined that so far as I am concerned, he shall never have cause to regret it."

In May, Aunt Margaretta surprised Charlotte with a visit. They attended the antislavery convention in Boston. There Charlotte was overjoyed to see the fugitive slave Anthony Burns. Now Burns was free. His freedom had been bought from his master in Virginia by a group of abolitionists. As a free man, Burns had hastened back to Boston to resume his work as a Baptist minister. "It's like a story in a book," Charlotte exclaimed, "a story with a happy ending."

All during the summer of 1855 Charlotte thought about September 12, when school would reopen. She was looking forward to it, and yet she wasn't, for the girls at the Normal School had not been as friendly as had the girls at Higginson. Perhaps, she thought hopefully, things will be better this fall.

When school reopened, however, the situation was no different. If anything, it was worse. Some of the girls were kind and cordial to her in the schoolroom, but when she met them in the street, they wouldn't speak to her. "These," wrote Charlotte, "I can but regard now with scorn and contempt—once I liked them, believing them incapable of such meanness."

Other girls, although friendly in the classroom, gave her the tiniest greeting in town, as though they really didn't know her at all. "I, of course," said Charlotte, hurt and proud, "acknowledge no such recognition, and they soon cease entirely. . . . Oh, it is hard to go through life meeting contempt with contempt, hatred with hatred, fearing with too good reason, to love and trust anyone whose skin is white—however lovable, attractive, and congenial in seeming."

As an afterthought, she added, "My studies are my truest friends."

On the night that Charlotte made this entry in her journal she could not sleep. She knew that she wasn't being fair to such white friends as Miss Shepard, the poet Whittier, and certain abolitionists, who risked their fortunes, even their lives to help the black people. Nevertheless, she was truly hurt by her schoolmates' behavior. She tossed for hours in her bed, resentful and unhappy. Then as the gray fingers of dawn crept in her window, a feeling of calm flowed through her. She jumped out of bed, lit her candle, and added these words to her journal:

> It is wrong, it is ignoble to despair; let us labor earnestly and faithfully to acquire knowledge, to break down the barriers of prejudice and oppression. Let us take courage; never ceasing to work—hoping and believing that if not for us, for another generation there is a better, brighter day in store . . . when the rights of every colored man shall everywhere be acknowledged and respected, and he shall be treated as a *man* and a *brother*.

Charlotte carefully read over what she had written. Then she climbed back into bed, and fell peacefully asleep.

7. Has My Dream Come True?

"Smile! Stand straight," eighteen-year-old Charlotte commanded herself as she stood for the first time before her fourth-grade pupils at the Epes Grammar School in Salem. "Don't let them see that you are a little afraid of them."

Thirty pairs of lively young eyes stared at her with curiosity. Some of the eyes belonged to gentle nine-year-old girls who had brought flowers to their new teacher just as they had brought them to their old teacher. Other eyes were those of tough-looking boys who were as tall as she was. A few of these whispered together and snickered.

A thought crossed Charlotte's mind. Were they snickering because she was black—the only black person in the school? Quickly she put the thought away. She must not, she told herself, dwell so much upon her color. The only thing that mattered was that she be a good teacher who could make the children *want* to learn.

The Salem School Board had hired Charlotte even before she was graduated from Normal School. She was grateful because she was desperate for money. Her father had written only once since he had moved to Canada, and then he had sent her no money. She supposed that Uncle Purvis would help her, but she was ashamed to have her relatives know that her father was neglecting her. She had been forced to borrow from Mrs. Remond, who was dangerously ill. This illness was a great worry to Charlotte, for she truly loved the kind, intelligent woman whom she had come to look upon almost as her own mother.

In this year of 1856 the young teacher had other worries also. Everywhere the lot of her people, both free and slave, was growing more desperate. From Philadelphia Aunt Margaretta wrote that she and another teacher, because they were black, had been called insulting names and had been put off one of the new public horsecars.

In Kansas the struggle between the proslavery and the antislavery people had become so violent that the territory (it was not yet a state) was called "Bleeding Kansas." Humane people on both sides were frightened because the quarrel over slavery had reached such a dangerous state.

Charlotte and her antislavery friends found, however, one bright spot in this picture. While the Kansas strife was at its height, a new political party—the Republican party—held its first national convention and nominated for president the explorer John C. Frémont, an antislavery man. "Free soil, free speech, and Frémont" was the campaign cry of the Republicans. Keeping slavery out of the territories was their main issue.

Surely, Charlotte thought, an attractive and right-thinking man like Frémont would win over a dull, weak candidate like James Buchanan, whom the Democrats had nominated for president. But she was wrong. In November 1856 Buchanan was elected president of the United States. The slaveholders and their friends rejoiced. The antislavery people were unhappy. The day after the election *The Liberator* came out with black borders, in mourning for the nation. Charlotte silently handed the newspaper to Mr. Remond. He threw it to the floor.

"I don't want to see it," he said angrily, and stamped out of the room.

Charlotte sighed. Poor Mr. Remond. Mrs. Remond had died three months earlier. Since then he had been in a bad humor. "Mr. Remond's gloomy countenance gives me a fit of the blues regularly every evening after work," she wrote in her journal. Nevertheless, she had agreed to stay on at his house because Sarah Remond had begged her to.

Mr. Remond's disposition did not improve. He

was rude even when guests were present. One rainy night in March 1857, Charlotte, Charles and Sarah Remond, the Putnams, and Charlotte's brother Henry, who was visiting her before leaving to seek his fortune in California, were eating and talking at the dinner table. For dessert Charlotte brought in a walnut caramel pudding that she had spent the morning making.

"My, this pudding is delicious," said Mrs. Putnam after she had taken a bite. "Isn't it, Charles?"

"Well, it's pretty good, considering who made it," Remond answered grudgingly.

Charlotte pretended not to notice the remark. She was upset anyway, as they all were. On this very day the highest court in the land—the Supreme Court of the United States—had dealt every Negro in the nation a severe blow. It had rendered the Dred Scott decision.

Dred Scott was a slave who had been taken by his master into the free state of Illinois and later into the part of the Louisiana Territory where slavery was forbidden by an earlier law, the Missouri Compromise. Then when his master took him back to Missouri, Scott sued for his freedom on the ground that he had twice lived on free soil, and therefore was no longer a slave.

The case had gone all the way to the Supreme Court, which had decided that Scott, because he was a Negro, could not be a citizen of the United States. Therefore, he had no right to sue in a federal court. The Court also decreed that Congress had no right to prohibit slavery in the territories. A slave, said the Court, is a form of property and, since the Constitution protects property in the territories, slavery is legal in these areas.

"No Negro an American citizen? How can that be?" Charlotte asked indignantly. "Negroes have been considered citizens of some states for years. They've voted in elections. Why, in 1834 Uncle Purvis and Aunt Harriet went to Europe with a passport signed by the secretary of state. The passport stated that they were citizens of the United States. Of course we're citizens."

"The high and mighty Supreme Court says we're not citizens, so we're not," Mr. Remond said with a disagreeable laugh.

After the guests left, Charlotte went to the backyard to draw cold water from the well for her aching head. The next morning she was still unhappy, but she put the Dred Scott affair out of her mind and hurried to school.

Her pupils were restless. The boys threw spitballs. The girls whispered and giggled. None could multiply four times eight. At ten o'clock she gave up.

"Early recess," she said. In the schoolyard Charlotte played ball, drop the handkerchief, and tag with her pupils. They were surprised that Miss Forten could run so fast and laugh so gaily. When recess was over, they marched to their classroom and quietly began their English lesson—a composition on "Why I Like Springtime."

Charlotte had assigned that subject because she herself so loved to roam through meadows and woods, searching for spring's bright violets and anemones and all the lovely wild flowers of the region.

Then also, as the snows of winter disappeared, the antislavery meetings in Boston and the literary lectures at the Salem Lyceum again flourished. Charlotte managed to attend an amazing number of these, for they "fed her soul," she said.

In one week she heard lectures on the Greek poets by the famous philosopher-writer Ralph

Charlotte attended many antislavery meetings in Boston like this one held on the Common.

Waldo Emerson and lectures on the Italian poets by James Russell Lowell, the celebrated essayist and poet. "It is almost *too much* happiness to have heard *both*," Charlotte confided to her journal.

After an antislavery convention in Boston several months later, she went walking in the Boston Common with Susan B. Anthony, the tall, grim, courageous leader of the unpopular struggle for woman's rights, who was also an abolitionist. Charlotte was awed and inspired by Miss Anthony, but once back in Salem, she wrote, "Now that the pleasant excitement of the meetings is over, I feel *very, very* tired."

As the days passed, she felt even more weary. She could hardly get out of bed. Soon Sarah Remond had to call the doctor for the young teacher. He came, examined her lungs, and told her she must stop teaching at once. She must, for a while, live in the country where she could breathe pure air and rest.

A week later Charlotte, accompanied by Mrs. Putnam, left for Philadelphia and Byberry. It was steaming hot when they came out of the railroad station in Philadelphia.

"I'm perishing for some nice cold ice cream," said the slim, well-dressed Mrs. Putnam.

"So am I," answered Charlotte.

They saw an ice cream parlor across the street, went in, and sat down at a small table. A red-faced woman with frowsy hair who was scooping up ice cream behind a marble counter rushed over to them. "You two get up from there right now," she said angrily, "and get out. We don't serve niggers here."

Charlotte and Mrs. Putnam rose slowly. They held their heads high, but their cheeks burned as they walked out.

"Oh, Caroline, I'm so sorry," Charlotte murmured. "I had forgotten there were such places here. There's a better ice cream parlor down the street. Let's go there."

The second ice cream parlor had crisp white curtains and highly polished tables. A young waitress stood near the door. As Charlotte and Mrs. Putnam entered, she came over to them.

"I'm sorry," she said in a low voice. "Please do not even sit down. We are not allowed to serve colored people. Please leave."

"Oh, how terribly I felt," Charlotte confided to her journal. "Could say but few words. Mrs. Putnam told one of the people some wholesome truths. It is dreadful. Dreadful! I cannot stay in such a place. I long for New England."

When she had been in Byberry a few days, however, the peace and beauty of the farm made her forget the ugly prejudice she had met in Philadelphia. There were many pleasant things to do. She drove in the pony wagon down shady lanes with her Cousin Hattie and Mrs. Putnam. She jumped into the hay wagon with Charley, who was now a lively, intelligent youth of fifteen. Her favorite cousin, Robert, Jr., still a mischievous boy at twenty-three, took time off from his paper products business in Philadelphia to take her sailing on the river.

Her journal had happy entries, such as, "I do enjoy rambling over the fields, picking fruit and flowers, driving in the cows, making butter."

And, "We sat on the piazza enjoying the delicious moonlight. Aunt Sarah and the girls singing very prettily."

Toward the end of August Charlotte felt strong enough to return to Salem for another year of teaching. A small pile of letters was waiting for her at the Remonds. She riffled through them quickly. The one she was hoping for, from her father, was not there. That night she complained to her journal. "I have known little of a father's love. It is hard for me to bear. I have a loving heart, and I long for a parent's love—for the love of my only parent, but it seems denied to me. I know not why."

In December, with snow heavy on the rooftops, a letter came. Half fearfully she opened it. As she had feared, her father wrote that he was "utterly unable" to help her. The money he had inherited from grandfather was gone. He was terribly sorry. His letter ended in an unusual display of affection.

For a moment Charlotte stood motionless in the empty house, for the others were in Boston.

She was shocked that her father was so poor. Then her loving nature showed itself, and she said aloud, "Ah, if he had only confided this to me long ago, I would *never, never* have asked his assistance. Dear Father! he is sorely tried. I wish I could be of some assistance to him."

As she put the letter in its envelope, she saw a few hastily scrawled lines on the back page. "Within the next few months I am moving to England. Would you want to come there with me? Perhaps you can secure the position of governess, or some similar occupation."

England! To live where her dark skin would not bring her suffering. To live where she could use her talents as she wished. Her dream of years had come true.

Joy flooded through Charlotte. A happy shout burst from her lips. She whirled through room after room in a dance of wild gladness. Then suddenly she stopped, almost as though she had been jerked to a stop by a rope. The radiance drained from her face. She sank down in a chair and began to cry.

8. Dark Clouds

After Charlotte had cried for an hour, she felt better. Outside, the early winter darkness was falling. "Good," she thought, "I'll take a walk. Nobody will see that I've been crying."

She walked on and on, unmindful of the snowy paths beneath her feet. All she could think of was the reason she could not move to England. "I cannot go," she told herself. "I must stay here and do what I can to help my people. That is what I have dedicated my life to. It would be cowardly of me to run away from what they cannot escape."

She felt ashamed of her father. He was a free

man, born of free people, Grandfather Forten's son, but he was throwing down the torch that the brave old fighter for Negro rights had handed to him. He was deserting the slaves in their struggle for freedom, running away from the black man's battle.

Suddenly she felt very cold, and she hurried home and warmed herself at the wood stove in the kitchen. In the morning, she decided, she would go to the antislavery fair in Boston to cheer herself up. The fair was already crowded when she arrived. Close to the door was the table of articles arranged by Mrs. Stowe, the author of *Uncle Tom's Cabin*. Charlotte admired the statuettes by a French Negro artist, but they were beyond her purse. Across the room she saw the noted antislavery orator Wendell Phillips speaking with Massachusetts Senator Charles Sumner, long a defender of Negro rights. With unaccustomed boldness she went up to Mr. Phillips and introduced herself. His kindly face brightened and he held out his hand in a warm welcome.

Before she knew it, she was telling Phillips about her chance to live in England, and why she felt she could not do it. Phillips' blue eyes deepened with understanding.

"My dear," he said, "I cannot but applaud your decision to stay and share the fight. You owe this to the noble name you bear."

And Senator Sumner, who had listened to her with interest, added, "Miss Forten, since you are free, it is a particularly fine thing you do. It is more exalted to struggle for the freedom of others than for our own."

About the time Charlotte decided not to go to England with her father, Charles Remond became so unpleasant that she and Sarah could bear it no longer. They moved to the Putnams' house.

Charlotte was happier at the Putnams, but in the spring she fell ill. Again the doctor told her that she must give up teaching for a while, go to the country, and rest. But this time a stay at Byberry did not cure her. In March 1858, poor health forced her to resign her teaching post at the Salem school. When she left, a leading Salem newspaper wrote:

We are sorry to hear that Miss Charlotte L. Forten has been compelled by ill health to resign her position in the Epes Grammar School. . . . Miss Forten is a young lady of color. . . . She passed through the Higginson School for Girls with decided éclat, and subsequently entered the State Normal School, and graduated with success. In both these schools she had secured in no common degree, the respect and interest of her teachers and of her fellow pupils.

She was subsequently appointed by the school committee to the Epes Grammar School. . . . She was graciously received by the parents of the district and soon endeared herself to the pupils (white) under her charge. . . . Her services have given entire satisfaction to the Principal of the school and to the school committee.

Charlotte returned to a Philadelphia that reflected the growing national conflict over slavery. The violent hatred between those who opposed slavery and those who favored it so

John Brown (center) bends over his son who was
mortally wounded at Harpers Ferry.

blinded both groups that neither would listen
to reason. In Illinois, Abraham Lincoln, as
candidate for the United States Senate, warned,
"A house divided against itself cannot stand. I
believe this government cannot endure permanently half slave and half free."

In Virginia, a fanatical abolitionist named
John Brown, who had taken a prominent part

in the Bleeding Kansas tragedy, planned a rebellion of slaves with the aid of a few whites. In 1859, with a band of thirteen white men and five free Negroes, he seized the United States arsenal at Harpers Ferry, Virginia. Brown hoped to free the slaves in nearby regions and set up an abolitionist republic in the neighboring mountains. He was, however, captured by a detachment of the United States Marines. Brown was tried, convicted of murder and treason against the State of Virginia, and was hanged.

Northern abolitionists hailed John Brown as a hero and martyr. Southerners called him a dangerous criminal. The friction between the free states and the slave states grew worse.

In 1860 the Republican party nominated Abraham Lincoln for president. The Democratic party split over the slavery issue. This split gave the victory to the Republicans.

When Lincoln was elected, South Carolina seceded (withdrew) from the Union. The people in power in South Carolina were afraid that their "right" to own slaves would not be protected under the Republican administration. By the time Lincoln was inaugurated as president in March 1861, Alabama, Florida, Georgia, Mississippi, Louisiana, and Texas had also seceded from the Union for the same reason. All of them then joined together to form a new nation called the Confederate States of America. These states were later joined by Virginia, North Carolina, Arkansas, and Tennessee.

In April of 1861 Confederate soldiers fired on Fort Sumter, a United States fort in the harbor at Charleston, South Carolina. Thus began the dreadful and dreaded Civil War.

While her country was in such turmoil, Charlotte was also going through a difficult period, although from time to time she was able to return to teaching in Salem. For two and a half years she did not write a word in her journal. Then one June day in 1862, she picked up her journal and set down what had happened to her since January 1860.

"When I wrote last," she began, "on a bright lovely New Year's Day, I was here in old

Salem ... assisting my dear Miss Shepard with one of her classes, and at the same time studying, and reciting at the Normal School, Latin, French, and a little Algebra. Besides, I was taking German lessons. Now was I not busy? ... Yet it seems to me I was never so happy. I enjoyed life perfectly, and all the winter was strong and well.

"But when Spring came my health gave way. First, my eyesight failed me, and the German which I liked better than anything else had to be given up, and then all my other studies. I was obliged to stop teaching and go away. . . .

"Early in September I recommenced teaching, feeling quite well. But late in October I had a violent attack of lung fever which brought me very, very near the grave, and entirely unfitted me for further work. . . . I was obliged to return to Philadelphia."

Charlotte remembered that she was not happy that winter of 1861 in Philadelphia. "A weary winter I had there," she wrote, "unable to work, having but little congenial society, and suffering the many deprivations which all of our unhappy race must suffer in the so-called City of Brotherly Love. . . ."

In May 1861 Charlotte had gone to Byberry to see the cousin she loved best, Robert Purvis, Jr. She found him very ill with lung disease. "And all the beautiful summer I stayed there," she wrote, "trying to nurse and amuse him as well as I could. Robert seemed to improve as the summer advanced, and in the Fall I left him, to take charge of Aunt Margaretta's school in the city. A small school—but the children were mostly bright and interesting; and I was thankful to have anything to do."

Charlotte's hand trembled as she wrote the next sentence. "In March poor Robert died. When I witnessed the agony of the loving hearts around him, I wished that I could have been taken instead of him."

When Charlotte's spirits were at their lowest, she got a letter from Miss Shepard asking if she could teach in Salem for the summer. Charlotte accepted gladly, saying, "I had been longing so for a breath of New England air, for a glimpse of the sea, for a walk over our good old hills."

She had been in Salem some weeks when John G. Whittier invited her and Miss Shepard to visit him. So on a lovely summer day the two teachers found themselves on a train whirling northward across the shining Merrimack to the poet's home in Amesbury. A short walk from the station brought them to Whittier's home on Friend Street.

Whittier's pleasant cottage in Amesbury

The poet met them at the door. "His tall form had not lost its erectness," Charlotte noticed, "nor his eyes their fire, and the smile which occasionally brightened his somewhat sad face was still the sweetest [I] had ever seen." The small white house was very quiet and homelike, and when they entered and received the warm welcome of Whittier's sister, the two women felt the very spirit of peace descending. Pictures and books and flowers were everywhere. They spent the evening in quiet, cheerful talk.

As a little china clock on the mantel was striking nine, the poet's dark eyes suddenly brightened with a thought. He reached out and took Charlotte's hands in his own.

"Charlotte," he said with great earnestness, "thee should apply to the Port Royal Commission. There is great need for thy services among the freed people of the South Carolina Sea Islands. Great need."

The Port Royal Commission. The Sea Islands. The freed people. These were much talked about in antislavery circles. The islands were noted for their great plantations which produced the famous Sea Islands cotton, whose long, silky strands made beautiful and durable cloth. The North had rejoiced when the Union fleet had captured the islands and their principal town, Beaufort, on Port Royal Island. The Sea Islands were important because the Union army and navy planned to use them as a base from which to attack the Confederate forts that protected the important city of Charleston, South Carolina.

When the Union commanding general, with 12,000 soldiers, set up headquarters on the Sea Islands, he found a strange and difficult situation. Some 10,000 slaves remained in the Port Royal region, deserted by their masters who had fled to the mainland at the approach of the Union squadron. The slaves were wretchedly poor. Most of them felt scared and lost. They had never planned their own lives. Now they were suddenly cast adrift, and they did not know what to do.

The Sea Islands slaves were the most backward of all the Southern slaves. Isolated from the mainland, they had lived for generations with almost no contact with the outside world, not even with Negroes from other sections. They scarcely knew their white masters, for the climate was so unhealthy that the masters spent only part of the year on the islands.

Their speech, called Gullah, was a curious mixture of African and English words, which the Northern soldiers found hard to understand. In other parts of the South some slaves were occasionally taught to read and write and to become skilled workmen, such as carpenters or stone masons. On the Sea Islands a slave was expected only to labor in the cotton fields.

The Northern generals worried about these people. They asked: Could these ex-slaves be of service to the Northern armies? Could they be persuaded to harvest the valuable crops of cotton that the masters had left standing in the fields? Would they revenge themselves upon all whites for the wrongs done to them as slaves? Would they fight for their freedom?

The Union general, W. T. Sherman, urged the government in Washington to send special agents to the Sea Islands to take charge of the plantations and superintend the work of the blacks until these former slaves could provide for themselves.

The problem of the abandoned plantations was given to the Treasury Department in Washington. The secretary of the treasury realized that more was involved than a cotton crop and 10,000 deserted ex-slaves. Here, he thought, was a chance to show the Negroes' true ability. If the black people could be trained by skilled supervisors, taught by experienced teachers, and given some government help, he believed that they would prove to be as capable as any other people. He decided to make Port Royal the scene of an experiment of importance to the entire nation.

To direct the Port Royal experiment, the government chose Edward L. Pierce, a young abolitionist lawyer from Boston. Pierce selected superintendents to see that the crops on the abandoned plantations were properly cultivated and that the black workers were directed in their work and paid for their labor. Next he recruited teachers to teach the former slaves to read and write and to live in a style befitting a free people.

The government paid the superintendents, but the teachers had to depend upon the abolition societies for their salaries. The low pay did not bother the teachers like Charlotte Forten who were going to the Sea Islands only to help the people who so desperately needed their help.

Charlotte was accepted as one of more than fifty accredited agents of the Port Royal Relief Association. She was the only Negro. This, she thought, gave her great responsibility. She vowed to conduct herself so that the freed people would be proud of her.

Charlotte Forten as she appeared at the time of the Port Royal experiment

9. To the Sea Islands

On a warm, murky afternoon in late October 1862 Charlotte stood at the rail of the steamboat for her first view of the Carolina Sea Islands. She saw a long, low line of sandy points bordered by scrubby pine trees stretching out into the sea.

At Beaufort on Port Royal Island, Charlotte and her traveling companions, the Hunns, stepped gingerly from the boat onto the shaky wharf. A pleasant-looking woman came forward, her hands outstretched in greeting.

"I am Laura Towne," she said to Charlotte. "I am so glad that you are to teach in my school on Saint Helena Island."

Former slaves streaming into Union army lines.
Many of these freed people now lived in Beaufort.

"I am glad too," Charlotte answered sincerely, for she was instantly drawn to this calm-faced teacher, physician, and antislavery worker.

"While we wait for our boatmen to come for us," Miss Towne said, "we may as well look about Beaufort."

For an hour the little group wandered through the ancient town. Once it must have been a pleasant place, Charlotte decided, with spacious homes and streets lined with orange trees, live oaks, and sycamores.

Now over everything was an air of desolation, for the white inhabitants had fled when the Union forces captured the island. Fences were dilapidated, outbuildings tumbling down, the trees untrimmed, most of the houses empty and surrounded by piles of broken furniture and smashed bottles.

The only people on the streets were Union soldiers and the former slaves. Of these freed people Charlotte wrote:

> Women in bright-colored handkerchiefs, some carrying pails on their heads, were crossing the yards, busy with their morning work; children were playing and tumbling around them. On every face there was a look of serenity and cheerfulness. My heart gave a great throb of happiness as I looked at them and thought, "They are free! so long down-trodden, so long crushed to earth, but now in their old homes, forever free!" And I thanked God that I had lived to see this day.

At last the boat that was to take their group to St. Helena Island pulled up to the wharf. It was rowed by a crew of Negro boatmen. "The row was just at sunset," Charlotte wrote, "and the gorgeous clouds of crimson and gold were reflected in the waters below. Then as we glided along, the rich, sonorous tones of the boatmen broke upon the evening stillness."

Jesus make de blind to see
Jesus make de deaf to hear
Jesus make de cripple walk
Walk in, dear Jesus.

No man can hender me.

The young teacher found the short voyage "sweet and strange and solemn."

Miss Towne's carriage was waiting for them on the rickety wharf. "We had a long drive on the lonely roads in the dark night," Charlotte recalled. "How easy it would have been for guerrillas to seize and hang us, but we kept our spirits high by singing 'John Brown' with a will as we drove through the pines and palmettos."

After a night's rest and breakfast at the home of the superintendent of St. Helena Island, Miss Towne drove Charlotte and the Hunns to their future home, a deserted plantation named Oaklands. The young teacher was glad that John Hunn and his daughter Lizzie were going to live with her. She had become fond of them, but especially of Mr. Hunn, an elderly shabbily dressed Quaker who had been fined $3,000 in Delaware for sheltering an escaped slave. His mission now was to set up a store at which the freed people could buy household articles and clothing at low prices.

As they neared Oaklands, Charlotte studied the scenery. A sandy road, covered in low places with gleaming white crushed oyster shells wound among the cotton fields. Here and there were small frame houses, with narrow porches and four or five rooms, residences of former overseers. Rude pine-log cabins, leaning crazily in the bright sun, dotted the fields. These, Charlotte assumed, were the homes of the newly freed slaves. She noticed the palmetto trees standing lonely in the cotton fields like elms in a New England meadow.

The road leading to the plantation house was nearly choked with weeds. The house itself was in a rundown condition, and the yard and garden had a neglected look. But there were roses in bloom, feathery acacia blossoms nodded in the breeze, and the people she saw were friendly and polite.

Inside the house, Charlotte wondered what they were to do for furniture. The masters in their hasty flight had left their furniture, but much of it had been destroyed or taken by the Union soldiers who captured the islands. What was left had been removed by the free people, who, in Charlotte's opinion, had "the best right to it."

As she and Lizzie were looking around the empty rooms, an elderly former slave named Cupid appeared with a mule cart containing a bedstead, two bureaus, three small pine tables, and two chairs, one with a broken back. There were no mattresses. Suddenly Charlotte felt the chill in the October air and shivered.

"Don't you worry, Miss," the old man told her. "Cupid'll look after you." He went out and came back shortly with a load of firewood and soon had a cheery fire going in the fireplace.

While they were unpacking, they realized they

were hungry, but no provision seemed to have been made for their food. Then Amaretta appeared. She "was a neat-looking woman with the gayest of head-handkerchiefs and carrying in her apron a supply of eggs and hominy." With a smile, she announced that she would be their cook, washer and ironer.

"In a few days," Charlotte wrote later, "we began to look civilized . . . having made a carpet of red and black woolen plaid, originally intended for frocks and shirts, a cushion stuffed with cornhusks and covered with calico for a sofa, a table which Ben the carpenter made for us out of pine boards, and lastly some cornhusk mattresses which were a great luxury, after having endured agonies for several nights sleeping on the slats of a bedstead, covered with a blanket."

As a final home touch she hung up her favorite picture, *Evangeline*, and gathered some roses. To Charlotte a home without flowers was unthinkable.

Obtaining food remained a problem for all the

teachers. Hominy grits was their chief food. For breakfast they usually had grits, corn cake, coffee or tea, army bread when they could get it, and crackers when they couldn't. For lunch they had sardines, crackers, blackberries, in "pickin' time," and coffee. The menu for dinner usually was like breakfast, except that sweet potatoes were added. Occasionally the army sent them highly prized food from its own supply, such as molasses, sugar, dried beef, rice, and vinegar.

The freed people, although they had little themselves, made mealtime bearable for the Northern teachers. Charlotte found herself listening for a light tap on the back door, and then gladly accepting a gift of eggs or fish, wrapped in green leaves.

Sometimes the former slaves presented great delicacies to their new friends. Charlotte remembered feasting on watermelons, mellow figs, plump quails, delicate squirrels, fat rabbits, tender chickens, and shrimp and crab taken from nearby tidal creeks.

A few days after she arrived on St. Helena, Charlotte began the task she had come for—teaching the former slaves not only to read and write but to have respect for themselves and their race. She rode about the island on an old horse named Edisto, visiting each cabin and instructing the people in rules of health and cleanliness. She cut out dresses and flannel jackets for the old women and sewed garments for newborn babies. She helped with the sick.

Freed people of all ages studied at this school.

She poured out her loving heart to these people, and they responded with a devotion that sometimes moved her to tears.

Charlotte's school was held in the Baptist Church, a large brick building set in a grove of live oak trees dripping with long gray moss. Of 150 children, usually jumping and shrieking with excitement, 58 were placed in Charlotte's care.

At first she found school trying. "Part of my scholars," she wrote, "are very tiny—babies, I call them—and it is hard to keep them quiet and interested while I am hearing the larger ones. They are too young even for the alphabet. I think I must write home and ask somebody to send me picture books and toys to amuse them with. These little ones were brought to school because the older children—in whose care the parents leave them while at work—could not come without them. The older ones, during the summer, work in the fields from early morning until 11 or 12 o'clock, and then come into school, after their toil in the hot sun, as bright and as anxious to learn as ever."

As the weeks passed, Charlotte found she was able to keep the children fairly quiet, even the "babies." All loved to sing, and soon she had even the tiny ones singing their ABC's.

Teaching the older ones was a hardship. There were not enough books and slates, although the Freedmen's Relief Association had sent a good supply. Charlotte had to "exert her lungs far above their strength" to make herself heard, for more than a hundred children in several classes were reciting at the same time in the same room.

The children appeared not to suffer from the confusion. "Their eagerness and aptitude in learning to read surprises everyone," wrote one of Charlotte's fellow teachers. "Their memories are usually excellent, their power of observation keen. Of course there are some stupid ones, but these are in the minority. The majority learn with wonderful rapidity."

Mr. Pierce, the superintendent general, visited Charlotte's school several months after she arrived. He noted that her pupils could read easily from second-grade readers, and that some could even read the Bible. In arithmetic they were beginning on the sixes in the multiplication table.

Mr. Pierce also agreed with another teacher who said to him, "Miss Forten has one of the sweetest voices I ever heard. She is treated by the Negroes with universal respect. She is an educated lady."

Sometimes after the children had finished their regular school work, the teachers would tell them about some of the great and good men in history. One day Miss Towne told them the story of John Brown, "the brave old man who had died for them." Then she taught them the John Brown song. This soon became one of the children's favorites. "We'll hang Jeff Davis on a sour apple tree," they sang with spirit.

Charlotte had special stories for her pupils. "Talked to the children a little while today about the noble Toussaint [L'Ouverture]," she wrote in her journal. "They listened attentively. It is well that they should know what one of

The playground of a school for freed children

their own color could do for his race. I long to
inspire them with courage and ambition and
high purpose."

Often when darkness had fallen on the plantation, and Charlotte was reading by the light
of the oil lamp, there would be a gentle tap on
the front door. "It's Harry," she would say to
herself, jumping to her feet to let him in.

Harry was a tall, broad man in his thirties,
a field hand who wanted desperately to learn
to read and write. Since he had to work in the

fields during the day, the only time he had for lessons was at night.

"Harry is really a scholar to be proud of," Charlotte wrote. "He learns rapidly. I gave him his first lesson in writing tonight, and his progress was wonderful. He held the pen almost perfectly right the first time. . . . I must inquire if there are no more of the grown people who would like to take lessons at night. Whenever I am well enough, it will be a real happiness to me to teach them."

Soon Charlotte had a class of men and women who came to her at night. They traced their letters on their slates with stiff, toil-worn fingers. They read painfully from their children's schoolbooks, but they did read and they did write.

The young black school teacher from Philadelphia was proud of them.

10. The Tallest Tree in Paradise

On St. Helena Island, the freed people and the Northern teachers always went to church. Charlotte usually rode to the meeting in a buggy with Superintendent Soule and two other teachers. One of them described a Sunday gathering this way:

> The road to the Brick Church was crowded with a gaily dressed throng of black folk, some on foot, some on horseback, some in wagons, others in the rude ox-carts of plantation days. They were a colorful sight in their gaudy calicoes and crinolines. The younger women wore straw bonnets, corsets, and cotton gloves, but the grannies clung to their many-colored handkerchiefs and their loose gowns cut after the fashion of slavery days.

"It is well that the people come to church

Laura Towne, principal of Charlotte's school, often attended church with her on Sunday.

together," Superintendent Soule said, "for they have no way of telling the exact time."

Charlotte already knew that the freed people had no clocks. To indicate time they used such expressions as "when de fust fowl crow," "when de sun stan' straight ober head," "at frog peep," and "when fust star shine."

Inside the church, which had been the white people's church, the freed people listened attentively to the minister, an earnest New England abolitionist. Charlotte sat in sort of a trance and listened to the sermon, looking all the while through the open windows into the beautiful oaks with their moss drapery.

Then the singing began. Charlotte stopped looking out the window. She who had always loved music was enchanted by the music of the ex-slaves. "Wonderful, beautiful singing," she wrote in her journal, as she marveled at their talent.

After the church services, marriages were performed. Being able to choose their own husbands and wives without having to ask the master's permission was a great joy to the former slaves. Often Charlotte helped the bride make her wedding dress out of an old lace curtain, brightened with feathers and ribbons, from the former master's house.

Although the freed people attended regular services in the Brick Church, they saved their deepest feelings for the Praise House. Even in slavery days, the Praise House, which was just a larger Negro hut, was the special property of the black people. Here they were allowed to hold meetings without interference. After the masters fled, the former slaves kept the custom of the Praise House and gathered there on several week nights and on Sunday afternoons.

The Praise House meetings began, like the regular church services, with singing, praying, and preaching. When the religious services were over, the "Shout" began. The benches were pushed to the wall, and old and young men, women with gay handkerchiefs about their heads, and barefooted girls all stood up in the middle of the floor. When the spiritual was struck up, they began walking, then shuffling, faster and faster, round and round, one after the other in a ring.

"At the 'Shouts' the people sing their own songs," Charlotte wrote. "Maurice, an old blind man, leads the singing. . . . The large, gloomy room—the wild, whirling dance of the shouters —the crowds of dark, eager faces gathered around—the figure of the old blind man whose gestures while singing were very fine—and over all, the red glare of the burning pine-knot, which shed a circle of light around it—these all formed a wild, deeply strange, and deeply impressive picture, not soon to be forgotten."

Charlotte called Maurice's favorite song the grandest hymn she had ever heard.

> De tallest tree in Paradise
> De Christian calls de Tree of Life
> And I hope dat trumpet blow me home
> To my new Jerusalem.

"The tallest tree in Paradise"—the poet in her leaped at the words. They echoed in her mind for years after she left the Sea Islands.

Although Charlotte was kept busy on St. Helena, one day she had herself rowed to Beaufort to visit Harriet Tubman. This heroic woman had in 1849 escaped from slavery in Maryland. Not content with being free herself, she returned South at least nineteen times, risking her life to lead others to freedom. Now she was living in Beaufort, working among the freed people and serving the Union forces as both nurse and scout.

In Harriet's tiny cottage, Charlotte could

hardly believe her eyes. Could this frail, young-looking woman be the fierce fighter who had personally led over 300 slaves to Canada, forcing the timid ones ahead of her with a loaded revolver? Later, Charlotte was still marvelling as she wrote in her journal:

She [Harriet Tubman] told us that she used to hide the slaves in the woods during the day and go around to get provisions for them. Once she had with her a man named Joe, for whom a reward of $1500 was offered. Frequently, in different places she found handbills exactly describing him, but at last they reached in safety the Suspension Bridge over the Falls and found themselves in Canada. Until then, she said, Joe had been very silent. In vain she called his attention to the glory of the Falls. He sat perfectly still—moody, it seemed, and would not even glance at them. But when she said, "Now we are in Canada," he sprang to his feet with a great shout, and sang and clapped his hands in a perfect delirium of joy. So when they got out, and he first touched *free* soil, he shouted and hurrahed "as if he were crazy."

How exciting it was to hear her tell the story. . . . My own eyes were full as I listened to her—the heroic woman! A reward of $10,000 was offered for her by the Southerners, and her friends deemed it best that she should, for a time, find refuge in Canada. And she did so, but only for a short time. She came back and was soon at the good brave work again. . . . I am glad I saw her—*very* glad.

Harriet Tubman, daring conductor on the Underground Railroad and a brave Union army scout

One of the busiest places on St. Helena was Mr. Hunn's store, which he had set up in an outbuilding at Oaklands. From time to time Charlotte kept the store. She wrote about it this way: "Mr. Hunn's store was usually crowded, and Cupid was his most valuable assistant. Gay handkerchiefs for turbans, pots and kettles, and molasses were principally in demand. It was necessary to keep the molasses barrel in the yard, where Cupid presided over it and harangued and scolded the eager, noisy crowd collected around to his heart's content; while up the road leading to the house came constant processions of men, women, and children, carrying on their heads cans, jugs, pitchers, and even bottles—anything indeed that was capable of containing molasses.

"These people are exceedingly polite in their manner toward each other," she added, "each new arrival [in the store] bowing, scraping his feet, and shaking hands with the others, while there are constant greetings. . . . The children too are taught to be very polite to their elders, and it is the rarest thing to hear a disrespectful word from a child to his parent, or to any grown person. They have what New Englanders call 'beautiful manners.' "

One drizzly day in late November, Charlotte glanced at her calendar. "Mercy," she murmured, "Christmas will soon be here. I must write my Philadelphia friends and plead for some gifts for my little ones. And wouldn't it be wonderful if Mr. Whittier would write a Christmas hymn for our children to sing? Perhaps if I ask him . . ."

She dashed off a note and hurried out to catch the mail boat *Star of the South* that would soon be leaving the Sea Islands for the North.

The poet's answer came by return mail. He enclosed a "Christmas Hymn" that he had written especially for the children of the Sea Islands.

At school Charlotte showed the poet's picture to her pupils. "John Greenleaf Whittier is a very good friend of yours," she told them. "Let

us see how well we can sing the Christmas
hymn he has sent you."

The children learned the song quickly.

O None in all the world before
Were ever so glad as we!
We're free on Carolina's shore
We're all at home and free.

We hear no more the driver's horn,
No more the whip we fear.
This holy day that saw thee born
Was never half so dear.

The very oaks are greener clad,
The waters brighter smile;
O never shone a day so glad
On sweet St. Helen's Isle.

We praise thee in our songs today
To thee in prayer we call
Make swift the feet and straight the way
Of freedom unto all.

After school Charlotte went to her room and
sat up until midnight sewing by candlelight on
the little aprons she was making for each girl.

Christmas Day 1862 dawned bright. The
teachers were awakened early by the freed

people knocking on their windows and shouting "Merry Christmas." This was the signal for the teachers to proceed to the church that had been decorated with holly, pine, great pearls of mistletoe, and hanging moss. It looks very Christmasy, thought Charlotte, wondering how long the 150 children waiting there would remain halfway quiet.

Almost at once the teachers—Charlotte, Miss Towne, and Miss Murray—began handing out the gifts, most of which they had made themselves. Each girl got a dress, an apron, a sewing kit, and an orange. The boys were given shirts and pantaloons, and an orange. All happily received a picture book given by the abolitionist women of Philadelphia.

What a happy Christmas Day it was. Charlotte wrote, "There was cheerful sunshine without, lighting up the beautiful moss drapery of the oaks; and there were bright faces and glad hearts within. The long, dark night of the Past, with all its sorrows and fears, was forgotten; and for their Future—the eyes of these freed children see no clouds in it. It is full of sunlight, they think, and trust in it perfectly."

Before blowing out her candle that night, Charlotte's mind went to her loved ones far away. "Dear friends, up North!" she told her journal. "What would I not give for one look at your dear faces, one grasp of your kindly hands. Dear ones! I pray with my whole heart that this may have been to you a very, very happy Christmas."

11. "My Country! 'Tis of Thee"

January 1, 1863. New Year's Day. But never, thought Charlotte joyfully, had there been a New Year's Day like this, for this was Emancipation Day. This was the day that every slave in territory held by the Confederates became *officially* free—freed by decree of the president of the United States, Abraham Lincoln.

There was to be a great celebration at Camp Saxton, the camp of the First Regiment of the South Carolina Volunteers, which was made up entirely of former slaves. General Rufus Saxton, the present commander of the Military Department of the South, was sending his personal boat, the *Flora*, to bring the superintendents and the teachers to the festivities.

The sky was cloudless as Charlotte and the others climbed aboard the *Flora*. The ship was already crowded, she observed, with "an eager, wondering crowd of the freed people in their holiday attire, with the gayest of head-handkerchiefs, the whitest of aprons, the happiest of faces. The band was playing, the flags streaming, everybody talking merrily.

"The celebration took place in the beautiful grove of live oaks adjoining the camp. . . . As I sat on the stand and looked around on the various groups, I thought I had never seen a sight so beautiful. There were black soldiers in their blue coats and scarlet pantaloons, and crowds of lookers-on—men, women, and children, —under the trees. The faces of all wore a happy, expectant look."

There were prayers and poems, and then Dr. Will Brisbane, a South Carolinian who had freed his slaves several years before the war, read the Emancipation Proclamation with great feeling.

The cheers were still echoing as the military chaplain stepped up to the platform to present a beautiful American flag to Colonel T. W. Higginson for his regiment, the First South Carolina Volunteers.

Just as Colonel Higginson was taking the flag, "there unexpectedly arose close beside the platform a strong male voice into which two women's voices instantly blended.

> *My country! 'tis of thee*
> *Sweet land of liberty*
> *Of thee I sing.*

"People looked at each other and then at the platform to see where this interruption was coming from. Full of emotion the quavering voices sang on, verse after verse. Others of the colored people joined in."

"Just think of it," Colonel Higginson said later. "It was the first day they ever had a country, the first flag they had ever seen which promised anything to their people, the first time they were able to sing truly, 'My country! 'tis of thee.'"

The black soldiers who appeared on this Union army recruiting poster were typical of the proud men of the First South Carolina Volunteers.

Charlotte Forten, like many in the live oak grove, had tears in her eyes when the voices of the unknown singers died away. Her tears dried when Colonel Higginson, whom she had known in Massachusetts as the minister who had tried to rescue Anthony Burns, invited her and other dignitaries to dinner.

After dinner the First South Carolina Volunteers paraded for the visitors. "The long line of men in their brilliant uniforms, with bayonets gleaming in the sunlight, went through with the drill remarkably well," Charlotte wrote. "To me it was a grand triumph—that black regiment doing itself honor in the sight of the white officers, many of whom doubtless came to scoff. It was typical of what the race, so long downtrodden and degraded will yet achieve on this Continent."

It was dark when the teachers and superintendents climbed aboard the *Flora* for the trip back to St. Helena Island. All the way they promenaded on the deck in the bright moonlight, singing "John Brown," Whittier's "Hymn," and "My Country! 'Tis of Thee."

"Ah, what a grand, glorious day this has been," Charlotte wrote that night. "The dawn of freedom. . . . My soul is glad with an exceeding great gladness."

Three weeks after Emancipation Day, the First South Carolina Volunteers left on a dangerous mission. They were ordered up the St. Mary's River to capture Confederate supplies and cripple a vessel that was preparing to run the Union blockade.

As they crept behind Corporal Robert Sutton, who had lived in the region as a slave, rebel yells screeched through the woods. Rebel guns sprayed them with bullets. The black regiment returned the fire and held its ground. It returned with large quantities of bricks, railroad irons, a number of Confederate prisoners, and several rescued Negro families. Three of the men had saved the life of Colonel Higginson, and Corporal Sutton, although severely wounded, had refused to leave his post.

"My heart is filled with an exceeding great joy tonight," Charlotte told her journal. "The official report shows plainly how nobly and bravely the black soldiers can fight. I think the contemptuous white soldiers will cease to sneer very soon."

About the time the regiment of former slaves was formed in South Carolina, another Union regiment, made up of free Negroes, was organized in Massachusetts—the Fifty-fourth

Massachusetts Volunteers. By June 1863 this regiment, with its twenty-six-year-old white commander, Colonel Robert Gould Shaw, was encamped on St. Helena Island, waiting to take part in the attack on Charleston.

The attack on Charleston! A cold feeling slid down Charlotte's spine. She knew that this important Confederate port was stoutly defended. Everyone said that the rebels who held the forts in the harbor would die before they would surrender to the Union forces.

Early in July Superintendent-General Pierce invited Charlotte to go with him to visit the Fifty-fourth Massachusetts at its camp and to have tea with the officers. At the tea, Colonel Shaw, who knew of the proud reputation of the Forten family, came over to her, both hands extended in welcome. Charlotte was surprised by his appearance. He was so small, so delicate-looking. "Gentle, but brave and manly," she wrote.

And then on July 8, she added, "The regiment has gone. My heart-felt prayers go with them—for the men, for their noble, noble young Colonel. God bless him! God keep him in His care, and grant that his men may do nobly and prove themselves worthy of him."

Ten days went by, and the young school teacher waited anxiously for news of the Fifty-fourth Massachusetts. It was headed, she knew, for Morris Island where it was to join the attack on Fort Wagner, and so open Charleston harbor to an assault by the Union navy. Where was it now? What was it doing?

It was just as well that Charlotte could not see the black soldiers in the battle at Fort Wagner. Colonel Shaw had insisted that his regiment be placed in the forefront of the attack because, he explained, the men had begged for this place of honor and danger. Behind them were two brigades of white troops.

Darkness fell. The signal for attack was given. The soldiers started forward at double-quick time. They kept absolutely silent until they were within 200 yards of the fort. Then they burst into a yell and dashed forward into the

Confederate fire. Their headlong rush carried the Negro troops over the parapets into the fort itself. In fierce hand-to-hand combat they fought bravely, doggedly. But when the night ended, Fort Wagner was still in Southern hands. And the dead bodies of Colonel Shaw and more than half his men lay scattered over the battlefield.

In addition to those who died, many were wounded. There was a desperate need for nurses. Charlotte Forten answered the call. The

The storming of Fort Wagner by the brave troops of the Fifty-fourth Massachusetts Volunteers.

morning mists rose out of the river as she sat red-eyed and ill-looking in the boat that was taking her to the military hospital in Beaufort. Here hundreds of wounded soldiers lay unattended.

In the hospital, Charlotte helped wherever she was needed. She ran and ran, bringing medicines and bandages to the doctors. She went down the long rows of beds and pallets, speaking comfortingly to each wounded man and washing his face and hands. If he was unable to feed himself, she fed him and did anything else she could to help.

When she had time she wrote letters for the men and sewed up bullet holes and bayonet cuts in their pantaloons and jackets. The cheerful, uncomplaining spirit of the men amazed her. Their chief sorrow seemed to be that their gallant young colonel was dead. A young black soldier from Boston told her how Colonel Shaw had died.

"He sprang upon the parapet of the fort, Miss, and cried, 'Onward, my brave boys, onward.' Then he fell, pierced with wounds." The soldier's voice ended in a sob.

Although Charlotte said nothing to anyone, she was finding her hospital duties too much for her frail body. In the damp heat of the Carolina summer, the slightest activity wearied her. One day, as she was bringing a basin of water to wash a wounded man, she nearly fainted. A doctor saw her, took away the basin, and led her out under the trees where it was cooler.

He looked at her closely. "Miss Forten, I think you should go to your home in the North —before your health fails completely. Go before the fevers which abound here in late summer attack you. I don't believe you could survive a fever."

"But I am needed here," Charlotte protested.

"You can come back when the sickly season is over," he said firmly, "but now you *must leave.*"

12. Death of a Soldier

Word soon spread that Miss Forten had to leave the Sea Islands. The freed people crowded into Oaklands to help her get ready. Before the sun was straight overhead, they had her trunks in the mule cart, and the mule jogging along toward the dock for Hilton Head.

Charlotte just made her boat, the *Fulton*, which sailed into New York harbor three days later. She did not linger in New York but hurried to Philadelphia where grandmother and the others made a fuss over her. They brought her ice cream and made her rest on the sofa while she told them about the freed people on St. Helena. Charlotte noticed sadly that no one mentioned her father, but she understood why. Safe in England, the manager of a stationery store, he was the only one of James Forten's children who was not doing something to help his people in this time of crisis.

In a few days Uncle Purvis and Aunt Harriet came in their carriage and carried her off to Byberry. The big country house was quiet now, for Cousin Hattie was away raising money for a Negro college in Haiti, and twenty-year-old Charles, who had studied at Oberlin College for two years, was now an honor student at the Western Reserve Medical College in Cleveland.

As the lazy summer days passed, Charlotte's health improved. She journeyed to Salem to see her beloved teacher, Miss Shepard, and other friends of her schooldays there. She visited Whittier, went rowing with him up the flower-edged Artichoke River, and had tea and strawberries with him in his vine-covered cottage.

In October, when the weather cooled, Charlotte sailed back to South Carolina. As the low, flat shoreline came into view, she sat on deck and wrote, "I am once more nearing Port Royal. . . . I shall again tread the flower-skirted woodpaths of St. Helena, and dwell again among 'mine own people.' I shall gather my scholars about me, and see smiles of greeting break over their dusky faces. My heart sings a song of thanksgiving that even I am permitted to do something for a long-abused race, and aid in promoting a higher, holier, and happier life on the Sea Islands."

Four months later, in February 1864, pale sunlight slanted through the pines as Charlotte walked slowly up the path to the log cabin where forty lively pupils waited for her. She paid no attention to the cheerful chirping of the birds overhead. She could think only of the letter in her pocket—a letter from her father, written in haste from England.

She got out the letter and read it again. She still could hardly believe it! Father was coming back to his native land. He could no longer stand aloof from the battle of his people for freedom and for equality among men.

He was coming back to take part in that struggle, to lay down his life if necessary. He hoped that because of his superior education he would be allowed to be an officer in a black regiment, preferably a black regiment that was already at the front fighting the rebels. If he could not be an officer, Robert Forten wrote, he would enlist as a private.

Charlotte's eyes misted. Dear father. He was over fifty years old. It would be hard on him to be a front-line soldier. But she was proud of him, proud that he again was carrying the torch that Grandfather Forten had handed to him. She quickened her steps and smiled at how fast the children hushed their babble as she entered the schoolroom.

Several weeks later Charlotte again heard from her father. Existing laws prevented him from becoming an officer, he told her, so he was enlisting as a private in the Forty-third United States Colored Infantry Regiment.

Shortly afterward, there was another note. "No time to write," her father said. "Have been promoted to sergeant-major, and have been ordered to report to the chief mustering and recruiting officer of Maryland."

That note was the last word Charlotte ever received from her father. He died suddenly, in April 1864, of an infection he had picked up in one of the unsanitary army camps of the day. He was buried in Philadelphia in the family vault in the African Church of St. Thomas. Sixteen of his army comrades formed a funeral escort and fired three volleys of musketry over his grave. This was the first time in the nation's history that a Negro was buried with full military honors.

Her father's death put a severe strain upon Charlotte's health. Again her doctor insisted that she leave the South. In May of 1864 she did so.

Long after the flat sandy shore had faded into the misty distance, Charlotte stood at the rail of her steamship and thought about her life with the people of the Sea Islands. She was proud that she had played a part in the important Port Royal Experiment. Her mind went to the freed men who, with their own money, were buying farms on land which only a short while ago they had tilled as slaves. She thought of the two thousand black children who were eagerly attending school, and of the hundreds of adults who came to classes at night.

In less than two years the most backward of American slaves had proved that they could and would work to support themselves as free men. Their children had shown not only that they could learn in school but that they could learn quickly. Could anyone doubt now, the young teacher asked herself, that black people were as capable of progress as white?

For a moment Charlotte gazed at the glittering water. Then, smiling, she pulled her journal from her workbag and wrote: "The waves are a rich, deep green, the sky a lovely blue, the sun shines brightly, and it is very, very pleasant at sea. The Southern dream is over for a time. The real life of the Northlands begins again. [May it] Fare Well."

Afterword

When the Civil War ended, Charlotte Forten was only twenty-seven years old. She had made her way largely in a white society, had fought gallantly in the movement for the abolition of slavery, and on St. Helena Island had served her people in an hour of desperate need. Her later life, despite frequent illness, was one of continued service to her race.

After her return from the Sea Islands, Charlotte became secretary to the New England Freedmen's Aid Society, which sent teachers and other trained people into the South to help the former slaves adjust to freedom. She also added to her small salary by writing. Her earlier articles on the Sea Islands in the *Atlantic Monthly* had attracted much attention. Now she translated a French novel, *Madame Therése*, for the publishing firm of Scribners and wrote dozens of stories for a variety of magazines. However, her best work—articles which defended the Negro's character and progress—she contributed without pay to a number of Northern newspapers.

When the Freedmen's Aid Societies closed down, Charlotte moved to Washington, D.C. and became assistant to the principal of the newly-opened Sumner High School for Negroes. The principal, Richard Greener, was the first black graduate of Harvard University.

In 1878, when Charlotte was forty-one, she married the

Reverend Francis J. Grimké, the nephew of her old friends, the abolitionists Sarah and Angelina Grimké.

Francis Grimké was one of three brothers, two of whom had distinguished careers and became leaders of and spokesmen for the Negro people. They had been born slaves in Charleston, South Carolina, where their white father, Henry Grimké, belonged to an aristocratic Southern family. Their mother, Nancy West, was an intelligent slave.

Charlotte's husband was an outstanding graduate of the Princeton Theological Seminary. His sermons at the Fifteenth Street Presbyterian Church in Washington, D.C., where he was pastor, attracted nationwide attention. His brother Archibald, who was graduated with honors from the Harvard Law School, became a noted lawyer, diplomat, author, and never-tiring champion of Negro rights.

Charlotte and her husband had one daughter, whose death at the age of six months caused great sorrow.

The Grimké home was the gathering place for numerous outstanding Negroes living in Washington, D.C., including the black members of Congress who had been elected from the defeated Southern states after the war. One day in the Grimké parlor Charlotte watched her husband marry their good friend Frederick Douglass to his second wife.

Of her own family Charlotte saw most often her cousin Dr. Charles Purvis, who by 1882 was a full professor at the Howard University Medical School and head of Freedmen's Hospital.

She wrote regularly to Grandmother Forten who, nearly 100 years old, still lived with Aunt Margaretta in the big house in Philadelphia. Sometimes she heard from Sarah Remond who had studied medicine and become a successful doctor in Italy.

Charlotte never lost her love for books, paintings, and flowers. When her motherless niece, Archibald's daughter Angelina, came to live with her, she took the little girl regularly to the city's art galleries, the Library of Congress, and the Smithsonian Institution. Angelina grew up to be an outstanding poet and playwright.

In 1914, at seventy-six, Charlotte Forten Grimké died. She was mourned by thousands as a humane, creative, wise, and *strong* woman whose life was devoted to showing clearly and plainly the fine qualities of her people.

Her grieving husband missed her most of all. "She was," he said, "sweet and gentle, yet a woman of great strength of character. She had a bright and sunny disposition. She never grew old in spirit—she was always young, young as the youngest."

And her niece Angelina Weld Grimké created for her a loving poem, the final verse of which reads:

Where has she gone? And who is there to say?
But this we know: her gentle spirit moves
And is where beauty never wanes,
Perchance by other streams, mid other groves:
And to us here, ah! she remains
A lovely memory
Until Eternity:
She came, she loved, and she went away.

Index

"A Parting Hymn," 59–61
African Episcopal Church of
St. Thomas, 15, 138

Beaufort, S. C., 92, 97, 98,
115, 132
Brown, John, 85 (pic), 85–
86
Brown, William Wells, 51–
53, 59, 60 (pic)
Burns, Anthony, 41–44, 42
(pic), 65
Byberry, 17–20, 22, 76, 78,
83, 88, 135

"Christmas Hymn," 119–120
Church, Lizzie, 47, 54

Douglass, Frederick, 32 (pic),
141
Dred Scott decision, 72–74

Edwards, Richard, 62, 64

Fifty-fourth Massachusetts
Volunteers, 128–129,
130–132, 131 (pic)
First South Carolina Volunteers, 123, 125, 126–127
Fort Wagner, 130–132, 131
(pic)
Forten, Charlotte
at Byberry, 18–22, 78–79,
83, 89, 135
childhood of, 7–35
daughter of, 142
death of, 142
at Higginson School, 39–
61
and journal, 40, 43–44, 45,
47, 48, 49, 54, 55, 66–67,
78–79, 87–89, 90–91, 99
and marriage, 141
in Philadelphia, 7–17, 25–
35, 84–88, 134
and reading, 29–30, 56–57
in Salem, 36–76, 79–84

at Salem Normal School,
62–67
at Sea Islands, 96 (pic),
97–133, 136–138
as teacher at Epes Gram-
mar School, 68–76,
79–84
as teacher of freed people,
106–110
as writer, 140
Forten, Henry, 7, 8, 25, 27,
72
Forten, James, Sr., 8, 9 (pic),
10, 11, 12, 13–14, 15, 16,
20, 21, 57, 82
Forten, Mrs. James, Sr., 7,
10, 12, 23, 25, 34, 55,
62, 141
Forten, James, Jr., 16
Forten, Margaretta, 11, 12,
16, 25, 27, 28, 29, 31,
34–35, 55, 65, 70, 89,
141
Forten, Robert Bridges, 10,
16, 17, 22–24, 25, 27,
28, 34, 37, 39, 40, 43,
46, 50, 51, 61, 62, 69,
79–82, 136–138
Forten, Mrs. Robert Bridges,
11, 17
Forten, Robert Bridges, Jr.,
10
Forten, Sarah, 9, 16, 29, 31
Forten, Thomas, 25
Forten, William, 25
Forty-third United States
Colored Infantry Regi-
ment, 137
Fugitive Slave Act, 33–34,
35 (pic), 41, 52

Garrison, William Lloyd, 20,
30, 43–44
Grimké, Angelina, 31, 141
Grimké, Angelina Weld, 142
Grimké, Charlotte Forten
(Mrs. Francis J.
Grimké). See Forten,
Charlotte
Grimké, Francis J., 141–142
Grimké, Sarah, 31, 141

Higginson School, 35, 38, 57, 58–61, 65
Higginson, Thomas Wentworth, 42, 43, 125–126, 128
Hunn, John, 97, 100, 101, 117–118
Hunn, Lizzie, 97, 100, 102

The Liberator, 20, 43, 47, 56 (pic), 57, 71
Lincoln, Abraham, 85, 86–87

New England Freedmen's Aid Society, 140
New York Anti-Slavery Society, 52
The North Star, 32

Philadelphia Female Anti-Slavery Society, 31–33
Phillips, Wendell, 82–83
Pierce, Edward L., 94, 107–108, 129
Port Royal Commission, 91
Port Royal Island, 92, 94, 97
Port Royal Relief Association, 95
Purvis, Charles, 7, 8, 11, 18, 78, 135
Purvis, Harriet Forten (Mrs. Robert Purvis, Sr.), 17, 18, 19, 29, 73, 135
Purvis, Hattie, 7, 8, 11, 18, 19, 33, 78, 135
Purvis, Robert, Sr., 10, 17, 18 (pic), 19, 20, 21, 30, 69, 73, 135
Purvis, Robert, Jr., 7, 8, 10, 11, 18, 19, 78, 89
Putnam, Caroline, 43, 49, 76–78

Remond, Charles, 35, 37, 53, 71, 72, 74, 83
Remond, Mrs. Charles, 38, 50, 54, 69, 71

Remond Hair Works, 38, 63 (pic)
Remond, Sarah, 35, 37, 38, 43, 71, 72, 76

Saint Helena Island, 97, 99, 100, 105, 111, 115, 117, 129, 140
  Baptist Church, 106
  Brick Church, 111, 112
  freed people at, 92–95, 99, 104
  school at, 106–110
Salem Normal School, 62, 65, 66, 68
Sea Islands, 91–95, 97–133, 135–138
Shaw, Robert Gould, 129, 130–131, 132–133
Shepard, Mary, 39, 47, 50, 54, 59, 63, 64, 66, 88, 89, 90, 135
Stowe, Harriet Beecher, 56, 82
Sumner, Charles, 82–83

Towne, Laura, 97–98, 108, 112 (pic), 121
Tubman, Harriet, 115–117, 117 (pic)

Uncle Tom's Cabin, 56, 82
Underground Railroad, 21
United States Supreme Court, 72, 73, 74

Vigilant Committee of Philadelphia, 21

Whittier John Greenleaf, 14, 29 (pic), 30, 66, 90 (pic), 90–91, 119
World Anti-Slavery Convention, 37

144